Heavenly Chats
with
Izzy
and
Nana

A Day in the Park
Nancy Elizabeth Gainor

Illustrated by Susan McCarter King

This is a work of fiction. All of the characters, names, incidents, organizations, and dialogue in this novel are either the products of the author's imagination or are used fictitiously.

WestBow Press books may be ordered through booksellers or by contacting:

WestBow Press
A Division of Thomas Nelson & Zondervan
1663 Liberty Drive
Bloomington, IN 47403
www.westbowpress.com
844-714-3454

Because of the dynamic nature of the Internet, any web addresses or links contained in this book may have changed since publication and may no longer be valid. The views expressed in this work are solely those of the author and do not necessarily reflect the views of the publisher, and the publisher hereby disclaims any responsibility for them.

Any people depicted in stock imagery provided by Getty Images are models, and such images are being used for illustrative purposes only.
Certain stock imagery © Getty Images.

Interior Image Credit: Susan McCarter King

Scriptures taken from the Holy Bible, New International Version®, NIV®. Copyright © 1973, 1978, 1984, 2011 by Biblica, Inc.™ Used by permission of Zondervan. All rights reserved worldwide. www.zondervan.com The "NIV" and "New International Version" are trademarks registered in the United States Patent and Trademark Office by Biblica, Inc.®

ISBN: 978-1-6642-2169-7 (sc)
ISBN: 978-1-6642-2170-3 (e)

Library of Congress Control Number: 2021901861

Print information available on the last page.

WestBow Press rev. date: 02/08/2021

WESTBOW
PRESS®
A DIVISION OF THOMAS NELSON
& ZONDERVAN

Dedication and Acknowledgement

As our family experienced the deaths of loved ones, our grandchildren generated complicated questions that needed to be addressed. Within this navigation of grief, these daunting concepts were hard to explain especially on the level a child could understand. It became apparent that a book about heaven intertwined with nature and scripture could tackle some difficult topics as well as expand upon the imagination of a child. Many of these questions and even the responses were actual comments made by our grandchildren. I believe it is important to affirm children's beliefs, encourage conversations about loss, and alleviate their fears with the reassurance of Christ's love for them.

I dedicate this book first and foremost to the grace, mercy, and sacrificial love of my Savior Jesus Christ. The prompting of the Holy Spirit, the gift of writing and the inspiration of the Bible culminated to create *Heavenly Chats*. Researching this information allowed me to grow as a Christian in my stance concerning the joy of entering the kingdom of heaven.

I honor and praise my collaborator and cousin Susan McCarter King. Susan has overcome cancer and served as an inspiration to many as she faced tribulation with deep faith and joy. She is one of the most courageous Christ followers I know, and He has given her an incredible artistic talent which she has utilized to bring this book to life. It is a true delight to work alongside this amazing woman.

My husband, John, is my stanch supporter who instills vision and love in every writing endeavor. I am so thankful to have him as a best friend and life partner. Our children and their spouses Mike, Haley, Brian, Laura, Dan, and Mary validated the need for this book and encouraged its completion. Our grandchildren Kendall, Clara, Grayson, Garrett, Hudson, Ford, Parker, and Jackson are my motivation to instill the legacy of Jesus' love and precious worth for each one.

Finally, I want to acknowledge the reinforcement of friends and family who purchase and share my books with others. Because of their support, this ministry extends beyond my circle and into the hands of those who need to hear God's word and apply it to to their lives.

God bless you!

Susan McCarter King

Dedication and Acknowledgement

I dedicate this book first and foremost to God who has been there for me through my darkest of days to my most beautiful ones. He has made me stronger than I could have ever imagined. He has blessed me with the gift of creativity and art which I am so honored to be collaborating with my beautiful and talented cousin, Nancy. This has been one of my bucket list items since I was a young girl.

I want to dedicate my first book to my incredible parents, Jack and Ann McCarter who were always there for me, encouraging me when I was only four to keep drawing my heart out. Their positive support was instrumental in achieving my degree in graphic design. I lost my Dad in 2018, which shook me to my core, but thank God every day for letting me have him for so long. Mom, thank you for being my best friend in the entire universe.

My handsome and compassionate son, Jackson has always stood by my side through the bad times and good. I have told him from the time he was a baby "You're the very best thing I ever did" and that is true to this day. He is my biggest cheerleader giving me constructive feedback and constantly amazing me with his huge heart for others.

Love and Blessings!

Table of Contents

Time Together

Ten year old Isabella Jones is a curious child. With shoulder length auburn hair and shining blue eyes, her fascination with nature began as a young child when her grandmother would push her in a stroller throughout their small midwestern town. She loves the vibrant colors of flowers, the gentle movement of a butterfly, and the playful antics of chipmunks, squirrels, and other wee creatures. In Sunday School class she is also curious about God. She prays and reads her Bible that Papa bought her when she was eight. She has many questions and is not afraid to ask them.

Today Isabella and Nana are packing a picnic lunch and are headed to their favorite spot, Willow Park. The basket is stuffed with Isabella's favorite treats: crunchy chicken salad, cheese, fruit, spicy molasses cookies and pink lemonade. Nana affectionately calls Isabella "Izzy". Ever since Izzy was little Nana would take her to this county park to learn about God's creation and to share stories. This "one-on-one" time is precious as Nana listens attentively to Izzy describing her activities, friend's adventures, and school accomplishments. Nana is a good listener and always encourages Izzy to speak her thoughts. They love each other very much.

Where is heaven and what is it like?

As Nana packs up the picnic leftovers, Izzy stretches out on the soft, red blanket and studies the feathery clouds. The radiant sun warms her face, and the mockingbird sings an assortment of repetitive songs. "Nana, I can look up and see the beautiful clouds and blue sky. At night I can see the bright stars and moon. Are the sky and universe part of heaven? What exactly does heaven look like?"

"Those are excellent questions, Izzy," Nana said with a smile. "I've often wondered those things myself. The Bible contains scattered hints about heaven. The disciple John even wrote about the visions of heaven God gave him. With those many pieces, we can only imagine what heaven is like It's a mystery."

"As far as the location of heaven that is a complicated answer. We live in a world where things can be measured in distance, weight, and temperature. God lives in a spiritual place where these measurements do not apply. So, we can't look into a telescope and see heaven or measure how many miles away it is. I think heaven is in a place and time we really can't explain until we see it for ourselves. The universe is billions of light years away from us, but the Bible is clear that when we die, we pass immediately from this life on earth into the presence of Christ. This makes me think it is close, like stepping into the next room. All I know is that I believe it truly exists. When I think about heaven, I use my creativity to picture the most beautiful place in the world with God on his mighty throne. I visualize Jesus telling me stories while the angels serenade him with hymns."

How do you imagine heaven?

Your child's answer:

_____

_____

_____

_____

_____

"I picture children laughing, puppies jumping, and lots of ice cream," Izzy responds.

"It sounds just like a place I would want to visit," chuckles Nana. "In the book of Revelation, the streets are paved with gold, the gates are made of pearl and the walls of precious jewels. You know how much I love sparkly jewelry, so it sounds perfect to me. Heaven is so much more than anything we could ever imagine."

Our citizenship is in heaven. And we eagerly await a Savior from there, the Lord Jesus Christ. (Philippians 3:20 NIV)

Jesus answered him, "Truly I tell you today you will be with me in paradise. (Luke 23:43 NIV)

The New Heaven and the new Earth (Revelation 21 NIV)

A Place for Us

Nana and Izzy spot their favorite place in the park, an immense playground complete with green slides, rock climbing wall, and a lookout tower. Nana climbs up the narrow, wooden steps to the crow's nest with Izzy close behind and here they can view the entire park. In the little space they giggle and point to the wonders they see far and wide.

"You know, Izzy, this reminds me of the fact that heaven is a real place. Jesus told his friends that they should not be sad that he was leaving. He was going to heaven to prepare a place especially for them and he would be back to get them. He also said his father's mansion had many rooms for us."

What do you like best about your room at home?

Your child's answer:

_____

_____

_____

_____

"I love all my stuffed animals. At night I spread them all around me and cover them with my pink quilt. It is so cozy, and they help me to sleep," explains Izzy.

"Trusting Jesus who loves me so much helps me sleep at night," Nana continues, "but I have to admit if I had an animal like your Curious George monkey that would help me, too."

Do not let your hearts be troubled. Trust in God; trust also in me. In my Father's house are many rooms; if it were not so, I would have told you. I am going there to prepare a place for you. And if I go and prepare a place for you, I will come back and take you to be with me that you also may be where I am." (John 14:1-3 NIV)

Nana and Izzy arrive at another favorite place in the park. As they pedal their bikes along slowly, they spot a group of boys kicking a soccer ball and jubilantly cheering when they score a goal. Ahead they watch an older boy expertly weaving side to side with his jet-black skateboard and bright orange helmet.

Sporting a red top and purple shorts, a jogger swiftly passes them smiling with her head bobbing as she listens to music. On the basketball court, some girls shoot hoops and give each other high fives each time the ball swishes through the net. Taking a break from their ride, they pull over and quench their thirst with ice water stored in airtight thermoses. Adjusting her helmet, Izzy asks Nana, "Will there be fun things to do in heaven? Will I be bored?"

Nana looks around and says, "We have seen a lot of activity today. I believe we will be very busy in heaven as well. We will be worshiping, serving, learning, fellowshipping, and celebrating God while experiencing the most beautiful music ever heard. We won't even need earbuds to hear it. We will never be tired or bored. I know we will be busy."

What activities are your favorite?

Your child's answer:

_____

_____

_____

_____

Izzy thought for a moment. "I really like spending time with my family the most."

Nana replies, "Well that happens all the time in heaven as families are reunited. There is joy everywhere."

The throne of God and of the Lamb (Christ) will be in the city and his servants will serve him. (Revelation 22:3)

What will our bodies be like?

As they admire a garden of milkweed and bright red zinnias, a beautiful monarch butterfly catches them by surprise. "Look at the black spots in the design of that pretty monarch's wings," exclaims Izzy.

"Yes," responds Nana. "it's hard to believe this delicate butterfly was once a plain green caterpillar. Have you ever seen a caterpillar that spins itself into a chrysalis or cocoon?"

"Our teacher brought one into our classroom and we watched it break out of the cocoon. The class went outside, and we watched it fly away. It was so amazing," explained Izzy.

"The butterfly is a symbol of the resurrection. Christ died on the cross, was buried in the tomb which is like the cocoon. On the third day he was resurrected and began a new life just like the butterfly emerges and is set free. This is also a great way to think about the change in our bodies when we die. Our human bodies age and we can get sick and weak. When we die, we leave behind our old bodies and receive a new one much better than the one we had before. Our soul, or that part inside you that makes up your personality and who you are, lives on as you begin your new life in heaven. Because Jesus died for us, we can live again."

What do you think your new body will look like?

Your child's answer:

_____

_____

_____

_____

_____

"I hope I am tall with blonde hair and freckles. I've always wanted to have freckles," chimed Izzy. "But if I use my imagination my body would be like Jell-O and it would be designed with my favorite color."

Nana laughs, "I love you just the way you are my sweet granddaughter and the Bible states that we will have human bodies just like we do now. God has made each one of us unique, like every snowflake is different than any other snowflake. We will have that same one-of-a-kind identity when we go to heaven. No one else is exactly like us. Our bodies may not be perfect, but they will be naturally beautiful. Those who are handicapped will be able to run and play like you. After Jesus was resurrected, he looked like what he was before he died and that will be how it is with us."

For the trumpet will sound, the dead will be raised imperishable, and we will be changed. (1 Corinthians 15:52b)

Suddenly, the two are distracted by the soft sound of chirping above their heads. As Nana and Izzy gaze upward, they discover a bluebird's nest filled with newborn babies. The three tiny birds stretch out their necks, trying to grab the food that their mother has gathered. Mother bird is carefully placing worms in the open beaks of the hungry little ones. Father bird is circling above on guard to protect his precious family.

As she fingers her silver locket necklace, a tiny tear rolls down Izzy's cheek. "I really miss Pop Pop. I'm glad Mom Mom gave me this locket with his picture inside, so he is with me wherever I go. Some day when I am in heaven will he know who I am? I was little when he died, and I've grown so much since then. Do you think he visits with Great Grandma and Great Grandpa? I wonder if they are having fun talking about all the great grandchildren?"

Nana offers Izzy a big hug. "I miss them all so much. It is hard to have our loved ones die. It's comforting to know they are with Jesus, but we miss spending time with them. One thing that helps is to share stories about our life together. I especially like the memories that make us laugh. It's important to always talk about our loved ones so we will never forget how important they are in our lives."

"When we get to heaven, we will not only know our relatives, but we will also know many people there. Jesus calls his friends in heaven by name. So, you will be (your name) _____ _____ in heaven. There is proof of that in the story of the transfiguration. Peter, James and John recognized Moses and Elijah with Jesus and called them by name even though the patriarch and the prophet had been dead for hundreds of years. There was something about these men that made the disciples recognize them even though they had never seen them before. Therefore, I believe we will know people even if they have changed. In heaven there will be no strangers and we will have old and new friends."

"You will be the same there as you are here even if you are older. I am not sure what age we will all be, but I am confident that even if our bodies have changed, we will be recognized by those we love right away. Each one of us has a unique personality, memory, interests, abilities, and emotions that make up who we are. These things never change when you go to heaven. The place where we live may be different, but we are not."

Tell me a story about someone in heaven.

Your child's answer:

_____

_____

_____

_____

Izzy smiles and begins to share her memories of Pop Pop. "He was the best storyteller. He could make up tales that made us laugh about experiences he had when he was a boy. He loved to play baseball and he lived in a place he called the mansion at Rock Run that had lots of rooms and no heat. He told some great stories about his sisters too and he had some exciting adventures. I really miss him."

"Hearing stories of Pop Pop always makes me smile. You have a bit of his imagination in you," said Nana. "Let's get back on the bikes and continue our ride."

The story of the transfiguration (Matthew 17:1-9 NIV)

Are there animals in heaven?

With the wisp of fluffy clouds above and a gentle breeze brushing their faces the duo set off. As the trail curves, they witness a young girl being pulled by her yellow Labrador. "Who is taking who for a walk?" Izzy shouts.

"This is Buttercup and she thinks she is in charge," responds the girl with a sigh.

A few minutes later, they see a calico cat repeatedly jumping in the air, trying to catch an emerald dragonfly. Finally, she loses interest and curls up in the shade of a large oak tree to take a nap.

Izzy offers a sad smile. "I miss Gracie, my schnauzer. She always snuggled next to me at night, played ball with me in the yard and waged her tail when I came home from school. Are there animals in heaven, Nana?"

Nana thought for a moment and said, "All of God's creatures have a purpose. Many animals were intended for our enjoyment. If animals make us happy, then there is a place for them with us in heaven. In the book of Isaiah in God's future kingdom the wolf and lamb eat together. I believe this means man and animals will be together in the kingdom of God."

What do you picture your beloved pet is doing right now?

Your child's answer:

_____

_____

_____

_____

"I think Pop Pop is playing catch with Gracie. She loves chasing after the ball and he could really throw it far," Izzy answers and Nana grins as she pictures the two in paradise.

 The wolf and the lamb will feed together, and the lion will eat straw like the ox, and dust will be the serpent's food. They will neither harm nor destroy on all my holy mountain," says the Lord. (Isaiah 65:25 NIV)

In the distance Nana and Izzy hear the whimpering of a child. They race over to help a mother comforting her little boy with tears streaming down his face. He had been roller skating and fell, skinning his knee. Nana pours water out of her bottle onto a handkerchief and the mother gratefully places it on the cut.

"That should make it feel better until we can get you home and bandage it properly. Thank you," the appreciative mom said.

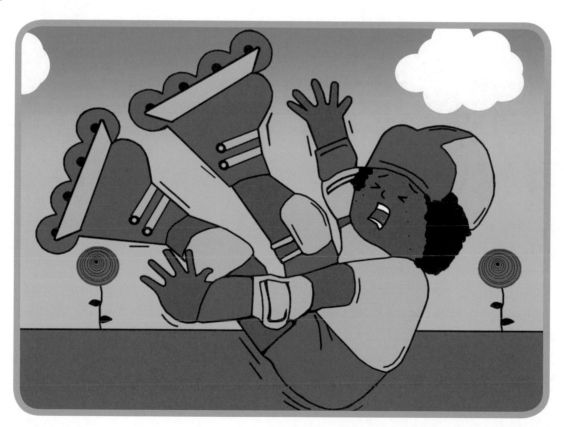

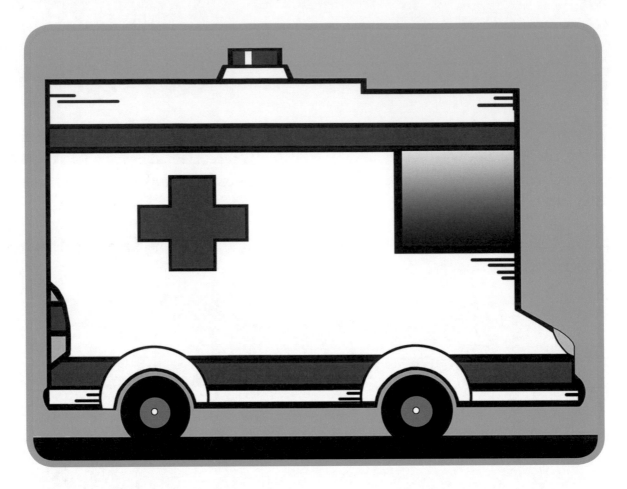

"You know Izzy, in heaven no one is hurt, sick or sad. Remember when we visited your friend Ella in the hospital?"

Izzy nodded. "Yes, she was extremely sick, and her parents were worried about her. Ella went to the hospital in an ambulance. The doctors were not sure what was wrong with her, but Ella was in lots of pain. That was a scary time for us. Now she is all better. I'm glad because we like to dance and have sleepovers." shares Izzy. Nana said, "Everyone in heaven is happy because they don't suffer from pain anymore."

Tell me an experience you had when you were sick or in pain."

Your child's answer:

_____

_____

_____

_____

"I remember the time I was running really fast on the driveway and fell. I had to get stitches in my chin. It really hurt for a while. Now I just have a little scar" describes Izzy.

"I recall that accident as well. You were so brave at the hospital when the doctor put in the stitches. I was proud of you," smiled Nana.

Blessed are you who hunger now, for you will be satisfied. Blessed are you who weep now, for you will laugh. Rejoice in that day and leap for joy, because great is your reward in heaven. (Luke 6:21,23 NIV)

He will wipe every tear from their eyes, and death shall be no more, neither shall there be mourning, nor crying, nor pain anymore, for the former things have passed away. (Revelation 21:4)

Returning from their fun but exhausting day at the park, Nana begins to prepare their tradition of afternoon tea. As the kettle whistles, Izzy sets the table with Great Grandma's fine china teacups, a pink floral tea pot and dainty shortbread cookies.

Nana loves afternoon tea. "The best part of a tea party," she tells Izzy, "is that we take time to talk about our day. We have to wait patiently as the tea steeps, but this means we have more time together without distractions."

The cinnamon and nutmeg aroma fills the room as the warm liquid is poured into the delicate porcelain. Izzy gingerly takes a bite out of the soft cookie. "These cookies are delicious but next time can we make our mini chocolate chip ones?"

"Of course, we can. We were so busy today we just didn't have time" said Nana.

"You know, Nana, I am always hungry, and I wonder will there be food in heaven, or will we eat clouds made with fruit and vegetables?" Izzy laughed.

"I believe there will be grand banquets overflowing with delicious food. The Bible mentions feasts, a marriage supper, and sharing communion with Jesus. When Jesus was resurrected, he ate fish with his friends. To me this demonstrates food will always be an important part of life in heaven."

What is your favorite food?

Your child's answer:

_____

_____

_____

_____

Izzy gleefully replies, "Dairy Queen Oreo blizzards hands down are my favorite! I could eat them every day."

Nana laughs, "Well perhaps we can go there tomorrow after school. For now, let's just chat about our day in the park."

Truly I say to you, I will not drink again of the fruit of the vine until that day when I drink it new in the kingdom of God. (Mark 14:25 NIV)

The resurrected Jesus ate. They gave him a piece of broiled fish, and he took it and ate before them. (Luke 24:42-43 NIV)

I tell you many will come from east and west and recline at the table with Abraham, Isaac, and Jacob in the kingdom of heaven. (Matthew 8:11 NIV)

Blessed are those who are invited to the marriage supper of the Lamb. (Revelation 19:9 NIV)

How do we get to heaven?

"Heaven sounds like a beautiful place, Nana, but how do we get there? I imagine that we step on a golden elevator and when the doors open, I see golden baby angels, trumpets and clouds covering everything." Izzy exclaimed.

Nana chuckles, " No one knows how we get to heaven or what we will see when we arrive there but we do have the promise of Jesus that we will arrive in heaven the day we die. When a person dies, the body appears to sleep but the spirit soars to heaven and the person is awake and ready to begin a new life."

Luke 23:43 Jesus answered him, truly I tell you, today you will be with me in paradise."

Nana goes to the family room bookshelf and pulls out her worn Bible. "As I turn these delicate pages it sounds like angel wings fluttering," Nana comments.

Scanning the pages Izzy notices that each is filled with notes and highlighted verses. "Why do you write in your Bible, Nana?"

"I highlight the verses that have special meaning to me, and I make notes of thoughts I have when I read them. To me it is like a school textbook I use to learn all I can about God. There was a time when I read the Bible cover to cover but that took me more than a year to complete."

As her hands rested upon the delicate page, Nana said, "I want to read you two verses that I love."

Jesus said, "I am the way and the truth and the life. No one comes to the Father except through me." (John 14:6 NIV)

Jesus said, "I am the door, if anyone enters through me, he shall be saved." (John 10:9 NIV)

"Jesus is the door to heaven, and he is the only way to get there," Nana explains. "Picture yourself standing at the gate of heaven with Jesus where you want to spend eternity. Why should you be able to enter? Many people think they can go to heaven because of all the good deeds they have accomplished. We do these things in life because we want to serve our Lord whom we love."

What good deeds have you done for others lately?

Your child's answer:

_____

_____

_____

_____

_____

"I took some candy to the nursing home residents on Christmas Day. I also made sandwiches to give to the food bank," replies Izzy.

"You are a girl with a big heart and lots of love for others. I'm proud of you," beams Nana.

"We can only go to heaven because we believe Jesus is our Savior who died on the cross for our sins. It is important to prepare our hearts now not later. Jesus is our hope for heaven, and we can always put our trust in him."

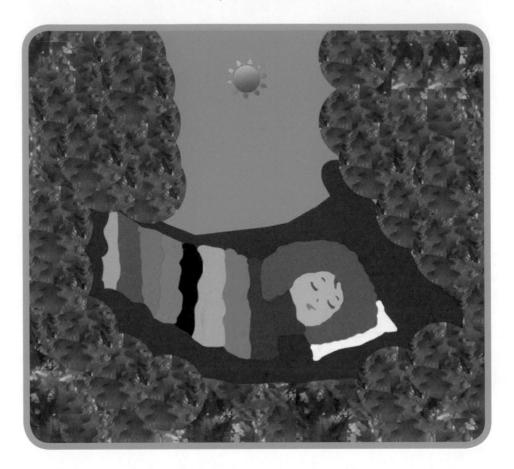

Izzy and Nana stroll into the lush backyard edged in red and purple petunias. The scent of freshly cut grass filters through the air. Abundant hostas border the pathway leading to the lavender hammock suspended between two stately Maple trees. Legs dangling from the corner of the woven cloth, they sway gradually side to side peering up at the clear blue sky. The bright sun peeks its rays from behind billowy clouds. Sparrows dart in and out of the branches heavily laden with crimson leaves. It is so peaceful!

"Thank you, Nana, for teaching me so much about heaven today. I had lots of questions and it was nice to have you take time to explain things to me," said Izzy.

"It was a memorable day. I love our time together. You are so precious to me," said Nana as she gives Izzy a bear hug.

What is the one thing that you learned about heaven that really stands out?

Your child's answer:

_____

_____

_____

_____

"I'm thinking a lot about that gate to heaven. I want to thank Jesus tonight in my prayers for loving me so much that he died for me. He must really care about me to make sure I will be with him forever."

"Our time on earth is a little like taking a trip. We make lots of stops along the way, meet new people, have wonderful experiences but our ultimate destination is heaven. With any trip we need to be prepared for a change in plans. Being prepared for heaven means telling Jesus about our sins, asking his forgiveness, and then thanking him for being our Savior. It's a simple but powerful conversation with your best friend."

What can I do for Jesus?

Izzy asks, "If Jesus did all the work to get me into heaven, what can I do for him?"

"Continue saying your prayers, reading your Bible and being kind to others. Your joyful spirit will draw others to him," said Nana.

"I love you, Nana."

"I love you more, my darling Izzy."

Printed in the United States
By Bookmasters